AF584450

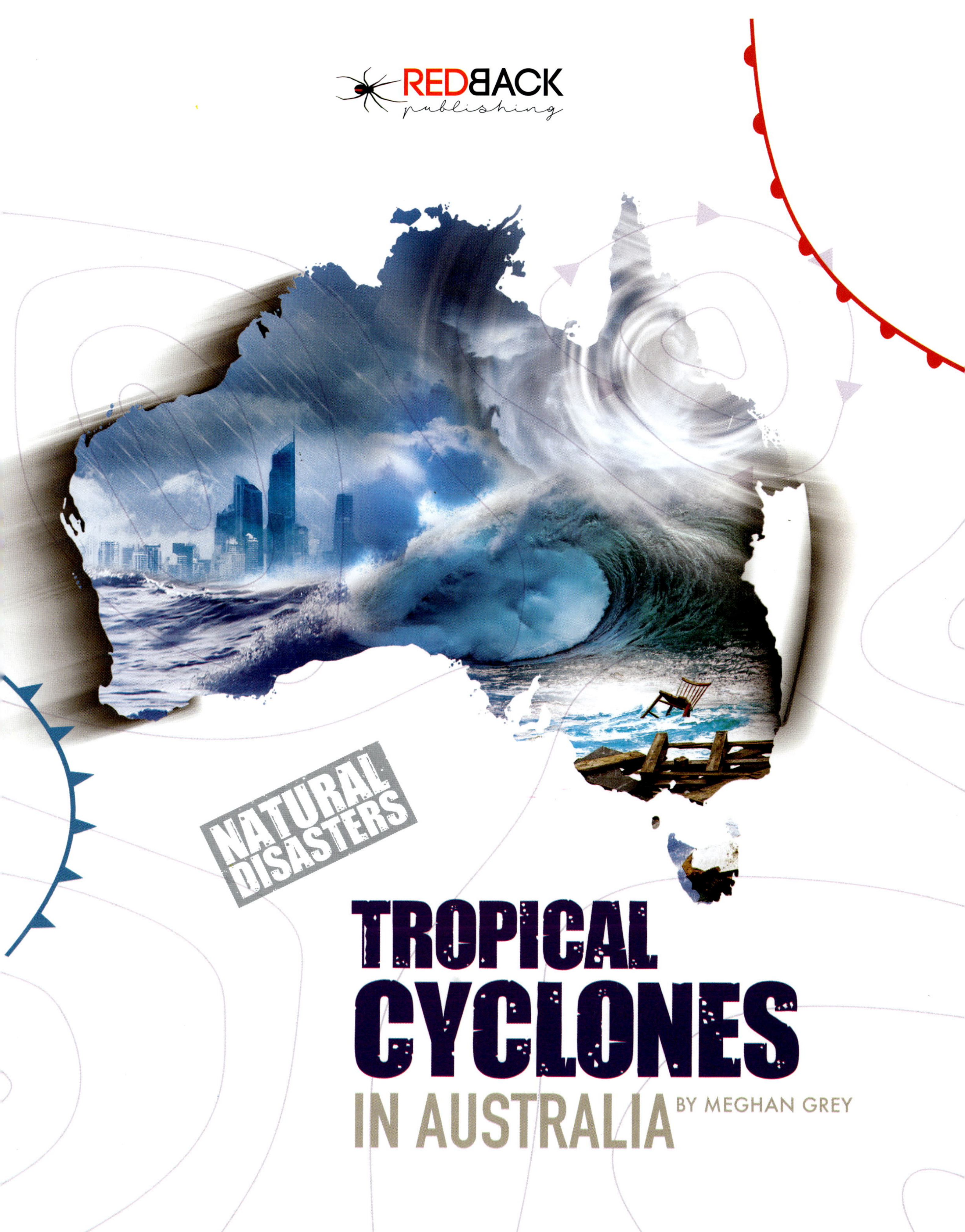
REDBACK
publishing
NATURAL DISASTERS
TROPICAL CYCLONES IN AUSTRALIA
BY MEGHAN GREY

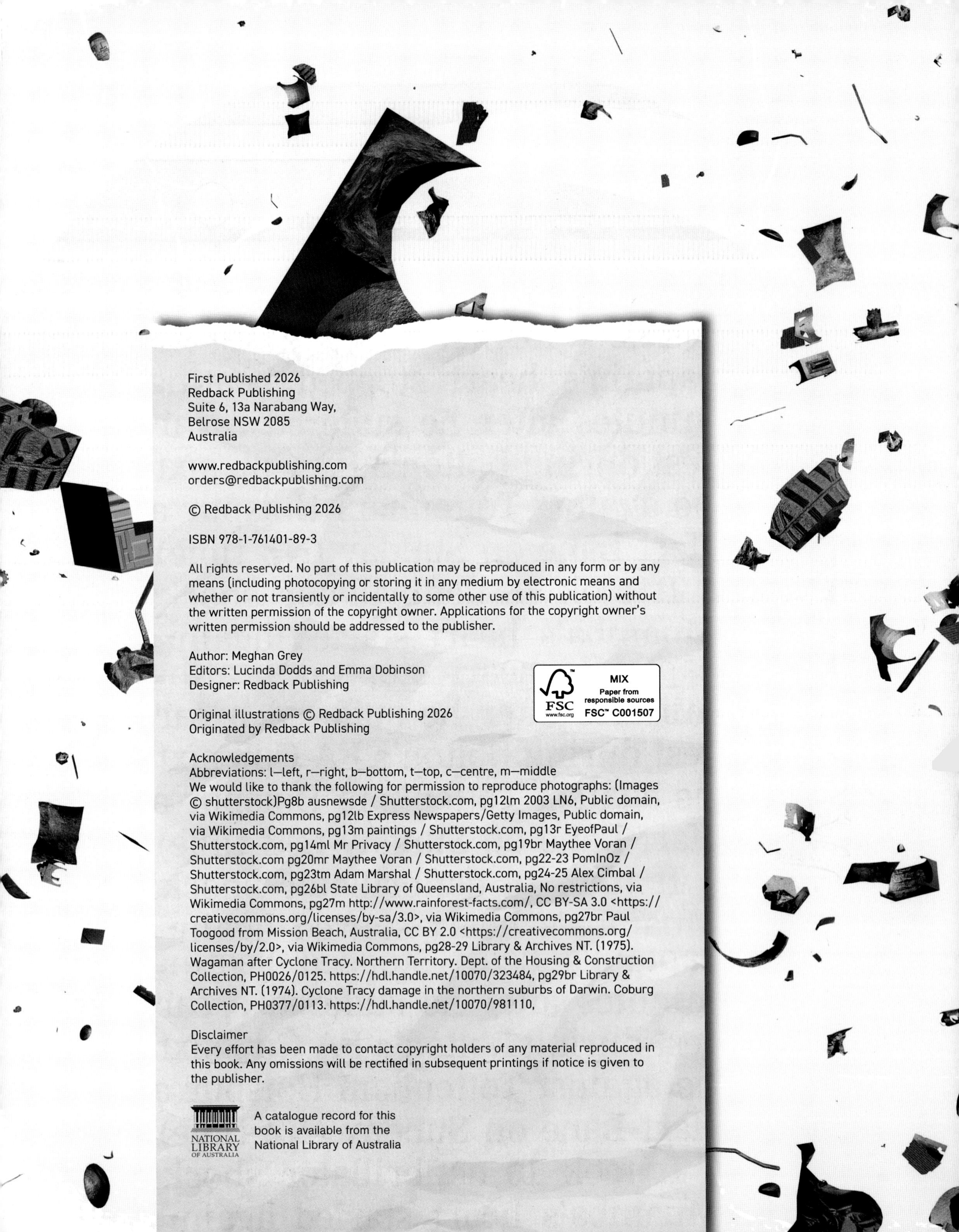

First Published 2026
Redback Publishing
Suite 6, 13a Narabang Way,
Belrose NSW 2085
Australia

www.redbackpublishing.com
orders@redbackpublishing.com

ISBN 978-1-761401-89-3

Author: Meghan Grey
Editors: Lucinda Dodds and Emma Dobinson
Designer: Redback Publishing

Original illustrations © Redback Publishing 2026
Originated by Redback Publishing

Acknowledgements
Abbreviations: l—left, r—right, b—bottom, t—top, c—centre, m—middle
We would like to thank the following for permission to reproduce photographs: (Images © shutterstock)Pg8b ausnewsde / Shutterstock.com, pg12lm 2003 LN6, Public domain, via Wikimedia Commons, pg12lb Express Newspapers/Getty Images, Public domain, via Wikimedia Commons, pg13m paintings / Shutterstock.com, pg13r EyeofPaul / Shutterstock.com, pg14ml Mr Privacy / Shutterstock.com, pg19br Maythee Voran / Shutterstock.com pg20mr Maythee Voran / Shutterstock.com, pg22-23 PomInOz / Shutterstock.com, pg23tm Adam Marshal / Shutterstock.com, pg24-25 Alex Cimbal / Shutterstock.com, pg26bl State Library of Queensland, Australia, No restrictions, via Wikimedia Commons, pg27m http://www.rainforest-facts.com/, CC BY-SA 3.0 <https://creativecommons.org/licenses/by-sa/3.0>, via Wikimedia Commons, pg27br Paul Toogood from Mission Beach, Australia, CC BY 2.0 <https://creativecommons.org/licenses/by/2.0>, via Wikimedia Commons, pg28-29 Library & Archives NT. (1975). Wagaman after Cyclone Tracy. Northern Territory. Dept. of the Housing & Construction Collection, PH0026/0125. https://hdl.handle.net/10070/323484, pg29br Library & Archives NT. (1974). Cyclone Tracy damage in the northern suburbs of Darwin. Coburg Collection, PH0377/0113. https://hdl.handle.net/10070/981110,

NATIONAL LIBRARY OF AUSTRALIA
A catalogue record for this book is available from the National Library of Australia

CONTENTS

WHAT IS A TROPICAL CYCLONE?

A tropical cyclone occurs when a circular storm system forms over the ocean in warm areas. The surface temperature of the sea needs to be around 26.5°C for this to happen.

These ferocious storms spiral inwards, bringing destructive wind and rain as they hit land. The force of a tropical cyclone can cause mass destruction. Statistics show that between 1998 and 2017, tropical cyclones caused more deaths worldwide than any other natural disaster other than earthquakes.

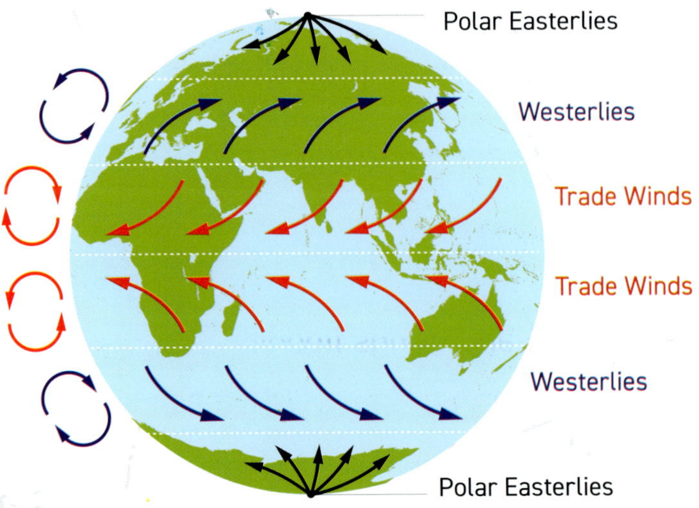

CYCLONE FACTS

In the northern hemisphere the winds blow anticlockwise.

In the southern hemisphere, the winds blow clockwise.

FAST FACT
About 400 cyclones have hit Australia's coasts in the past 70 years.

A TROPICAL CYCLONE DEVELOPS IN FOUR STAGES:

1. **Tropical disturbance:** a cluster of storms over the tropics.
2. **Tropical depression:** the storms now have circular winds. They can bring heavy rain, and cause flooding.
3. **Tropical storm:** once the low-pressure system has become self-sustaining it is named and classified as a tropical storm. A tropical storm can be damaging when it makes landfall and brings flooding.
4. **Tropical cyclone:** once the winds reach 62 to 88 kilometres per hour, the storm is a fully-fledged cyclone.

HOW A TROPICAL CYCLONE FORMS

In meteorology, a low-pressure system is one with moist, rising air that causes rain, storms and clouds. A low-pressure system is needed for a tropical cyclone to form.

4

The winds begin to blow in a circular pattern

3

The humid air cools as it rises, making large storm clouds

2

Winds are also needed to force the air up and outwards

1

Warm, moist air moves across the ocean causing water vapour to rise, acting as fuel for the storm

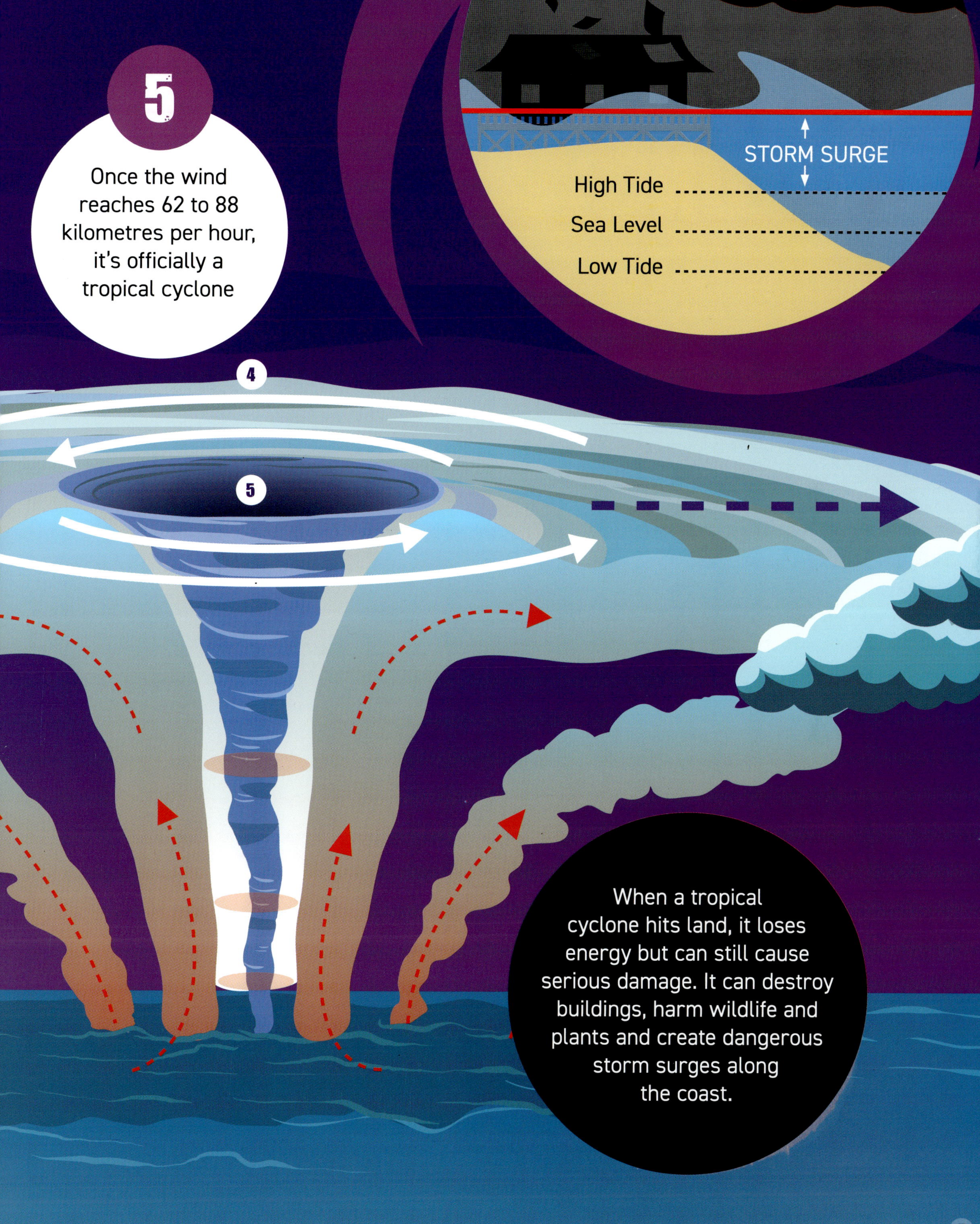

5
Once the wind reaches 62 to 88 kilometres per hour, it's officially a tropical cyclone
STORM SURGE
High Tide
Sea Level
Low Tide
4
5
When a tropical cyclone hits land, it loses energy but can still cause serious damage. It can destroy buildings, harm wildlife and plants and create dangerous storm surges along the coast.

WHERE DO TROPICAL CYCLONES OCCUR?

Tropical cyclones occur globally around the equator. Australia is one of the countries most impacted by tropical cyclones. They take place in regions with a monsoonal climate, such as northern Australia and the northwest of Western Australia.

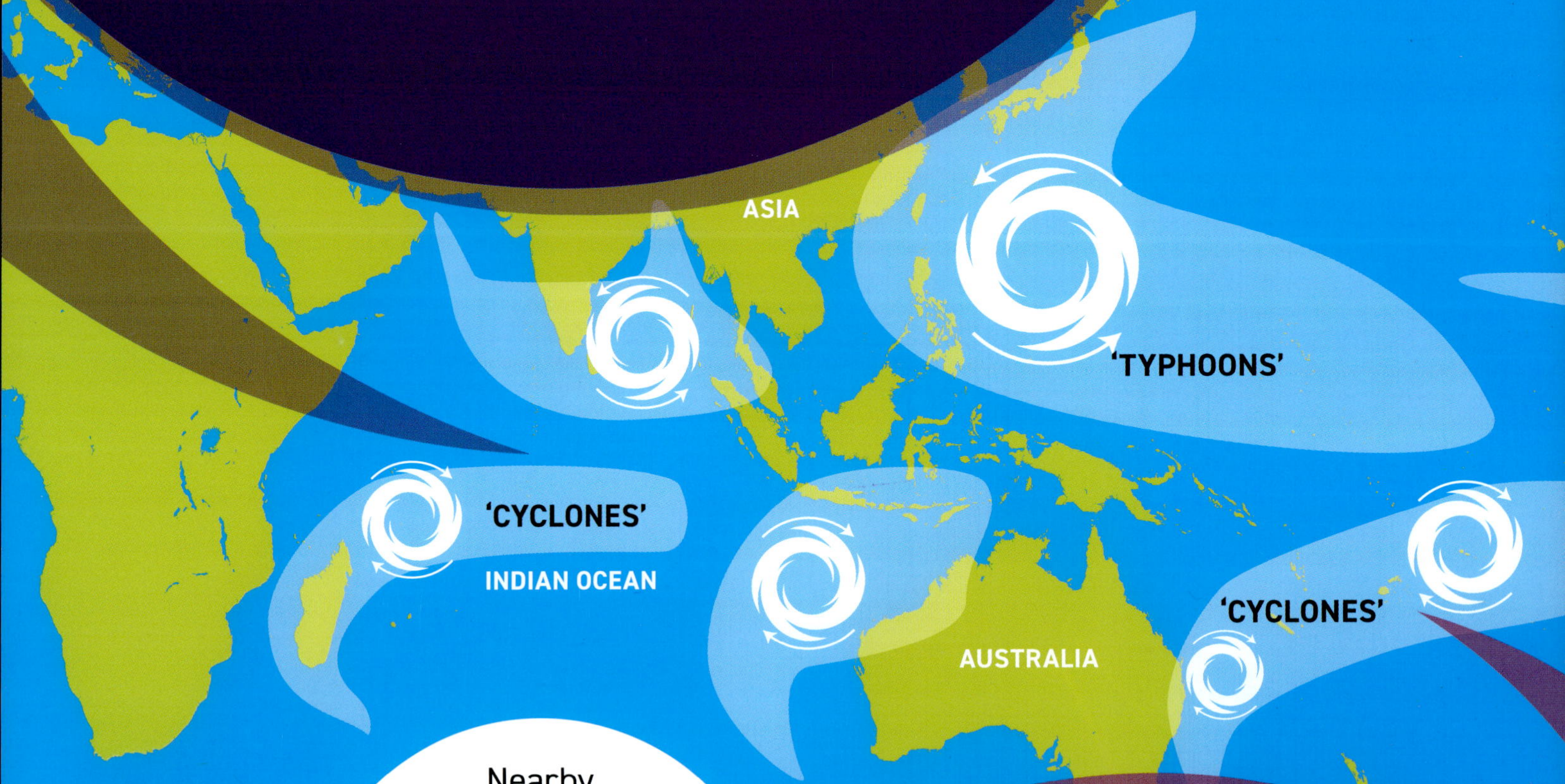

Nearby Pacific Island countries such as Tonga, Fiji, Vanuatu and Solomon Islands are in the South Pacific cyclone basin and experience regular devastating cyclones.

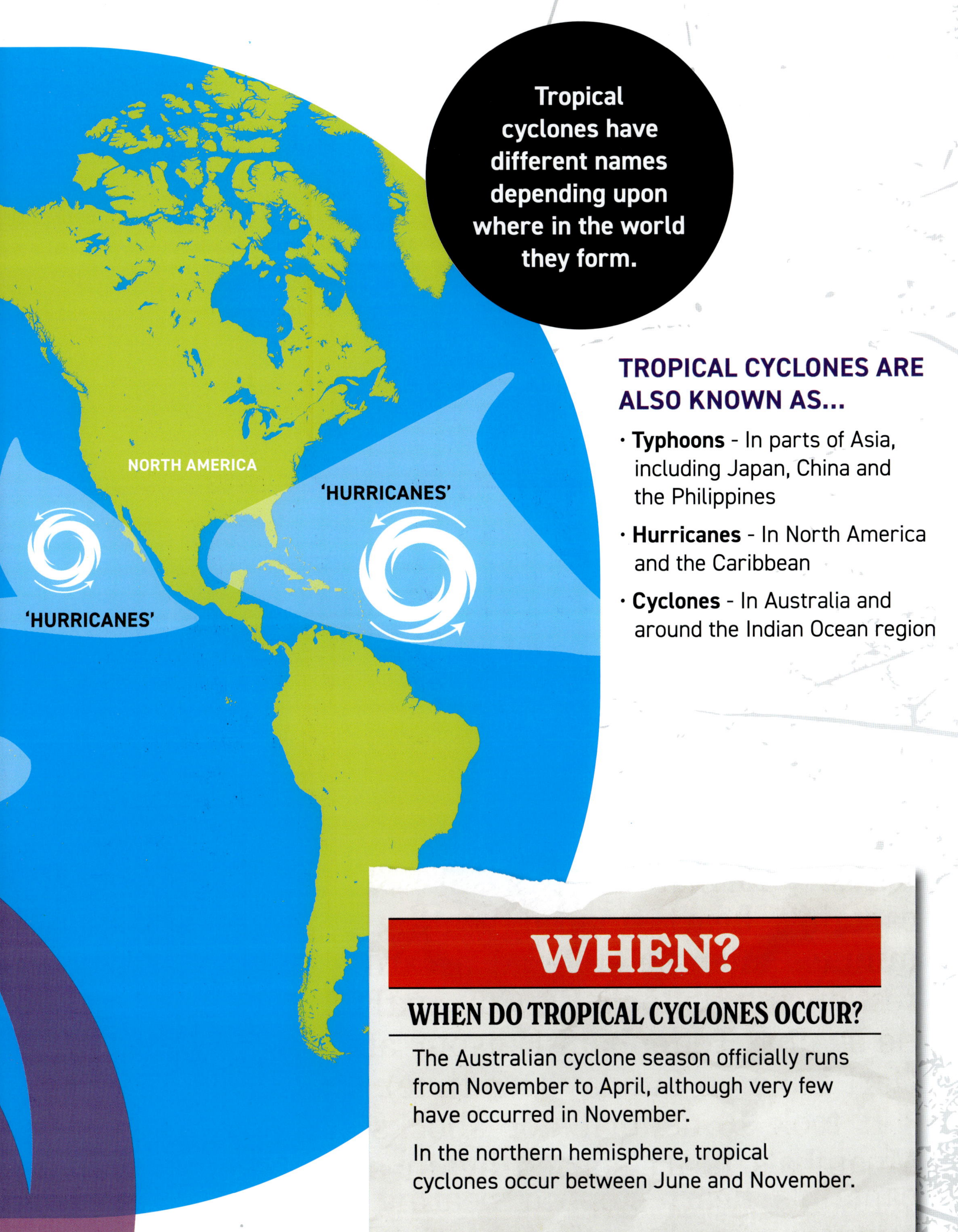

TROPICAL CYCLONES ARE ALSO KNOWN AS...

- **Typhoons** - In parts of Asia, including Japan, China and the Philippines
- **Hurricanes** - In North America and the Caribbean
- **Cyclones** - In Australia and around the Indian Ocean region

WHEN?

WHEN DO TROPICAL CYCLONES OCCUR?

The Australian cyclone season officially runs from November to April, although very few have occurred in November.

In the northern hemisphere, tropical cyclones occur between June and November.

FEATURES OF A TROPICAL CYCLONE

WIND

Tropical cyclones have gale force winds that do extensive damage to anything in their path. The winds hit in several ways, including gusts, downbursts, swirls and devastating horizontal winds. The strongest winds are near the centre.

RAIN

Tropical cyclones bring with them torrential rain. Known as rainbands, they spiral into the centre of the storm. Because of the moisture in the air, heavy rain can continue for days, even once the cyclone has passed.

EYE OF THE STORM

The centre of a tropical cyclone is mostly cloud free and an area of relative calm. This is called the eye of the storm and is generally around 40 kilometres wide. People are sometimes fooled into thinking the storm is over, but the eye of the storm means the cyclone is only half over. The winds that follow are often the strongest, generating in the area known as the eyewall.

THE EYEWALL

The strongest winds, heaviest rain and intense thunderstorms are found in the rainbands around the centre of the storm known as the eyewall.

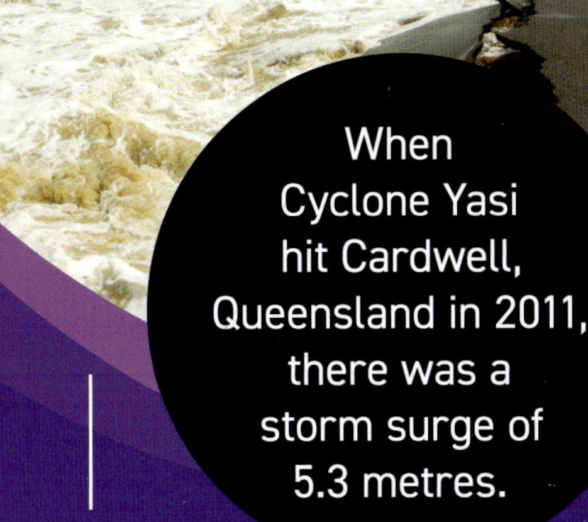

When Cyclone Yasi hit Cardwell, Queensland in 2011, there was a storm surge of 5.3 metres.

STORM SURGE

The winds produced by tropical cyclones can cause large seas, which damage the coastline and cause erosion. A storm surge is a rise in sea level that is typically about two to five metres higher than the normal tide level and can be up to 80 kilometres in length. If a storm surge coincides with a high tide, then dangerous fast waters will inundate the coast.

STORM TIDE

A storm tide is a tsunami-like body of water that hits the coast, when a high tide coincides with a storm surge. The height of a storm surge will depend on factors such as the speed of the cyclone, the angle of the sea floor and any funnelling effects of bays and estuaries.

DID YOU KNOW?

There are storm tide monitoring sites all along the Queensland coast.

TROPICAL CYCLONE CATEGORIES

Tropical cyclones are categorised between 1 and 5 according to their strength, with 5 being the most destructive.

In 1970, the Great Bhola Cyclone hit Bangladesh killing over half a million people.

CATEGORY 1

A Category 1 cyclone has gusts of wind up to 125 kilometres per hour. It will generally only cause minimal damage as it makes landfall.

CATEGORY 2

With winds often reaching 164 kilometres per hour, a Category 2 cyclone will cause damage to vegetation, street signs, caravans and small boats. It causes minor damage to buildings.

CATEGORY 3

A Category 3 cyclone causes significant damage as it reaches land, with winds up to 224 kilometres per hour. Power failures are likely from this category on.

CATEGORY 4

With winds between 225 and 279 kilometres per hour, these are very destructive cyclones, causing extensive damage to buildings and vegetation.

CATEGORY 5

With winds often more than 280 kilometres per hour, these are the most dangerous cyclones, causing widespread destruction. Ilsa was a recent Category 5 cyclone, forming off the coast of Western Australia in April 2023.

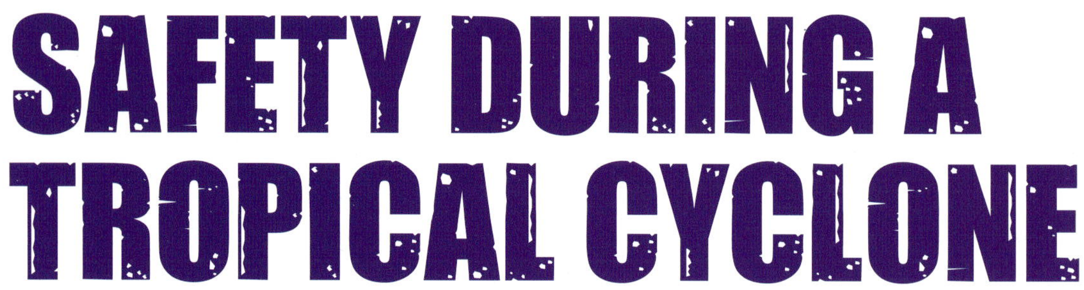

SAFETY DURING A TROPICAL CYCLONE

Preparation is key to staying safe during a tropical cyclone. The Australian Bureau of Meteorology (BoM) issues warnings and advice about extreme weather, including cyclones.

The BoM maintains watch across the region, reporting on seasonal outlooks for Australia and the South Pacific and providing forecasts.

STOCK UP!

EMERGENCY KIT ESSENTIALS

For those living in a cyclone-prone area, the following things should be maintained in an emergency kit:

- ☑ Water
- ☑ Canned food and a can opener
- ☑ A portable battery radio
- ☑ A torch and spare batteries
- ☑ Matches

Also make sure you have a first aid kit, and if possible a portable stove and eating utensils. Keep all your essentials in plastic bags in case they get wet.

LIVING IN AN AREA PRONE TO TROPICAL CYCLONES

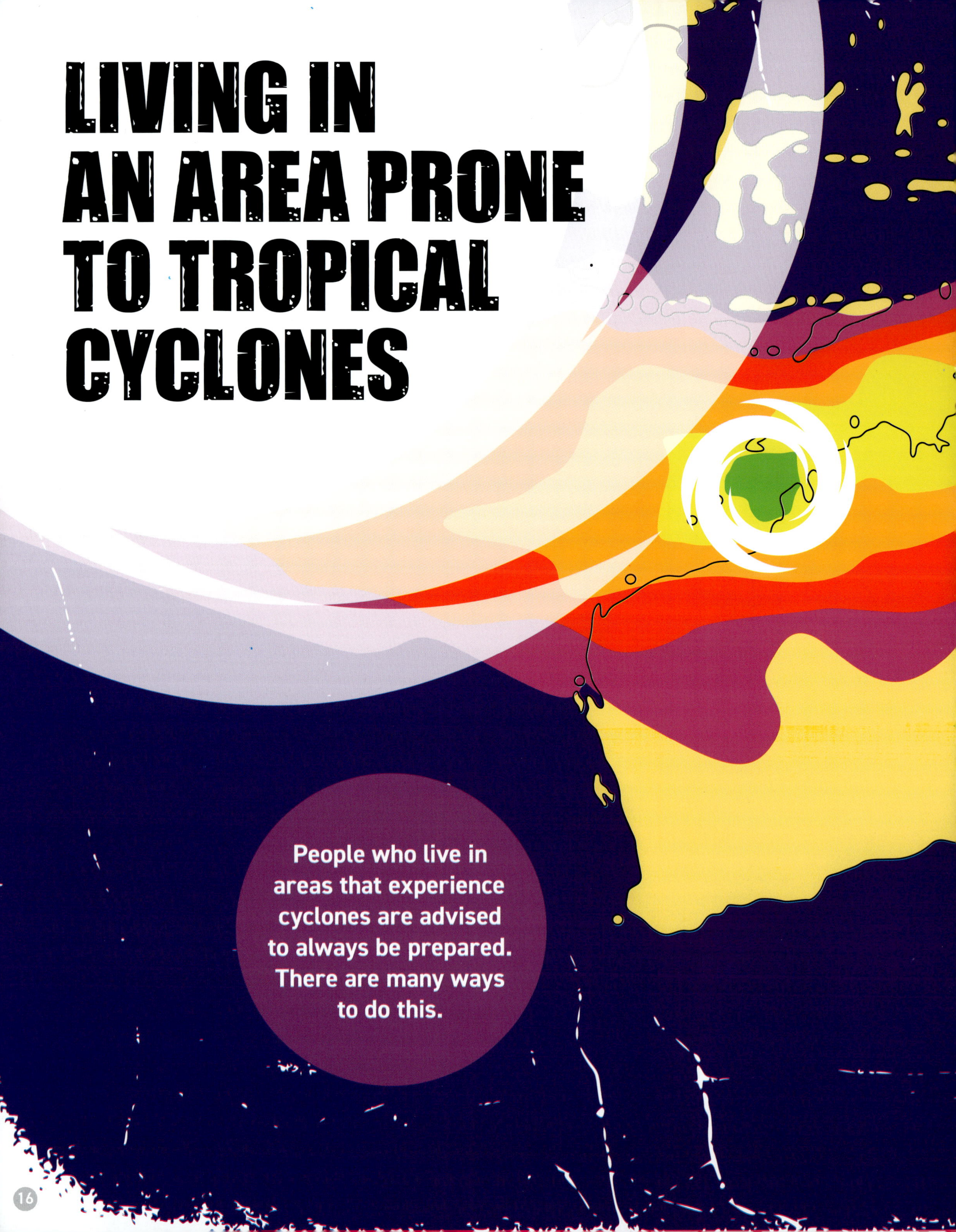

People who live in areas that experience cyclones are advised to always be prepared. There are many ways to do this.

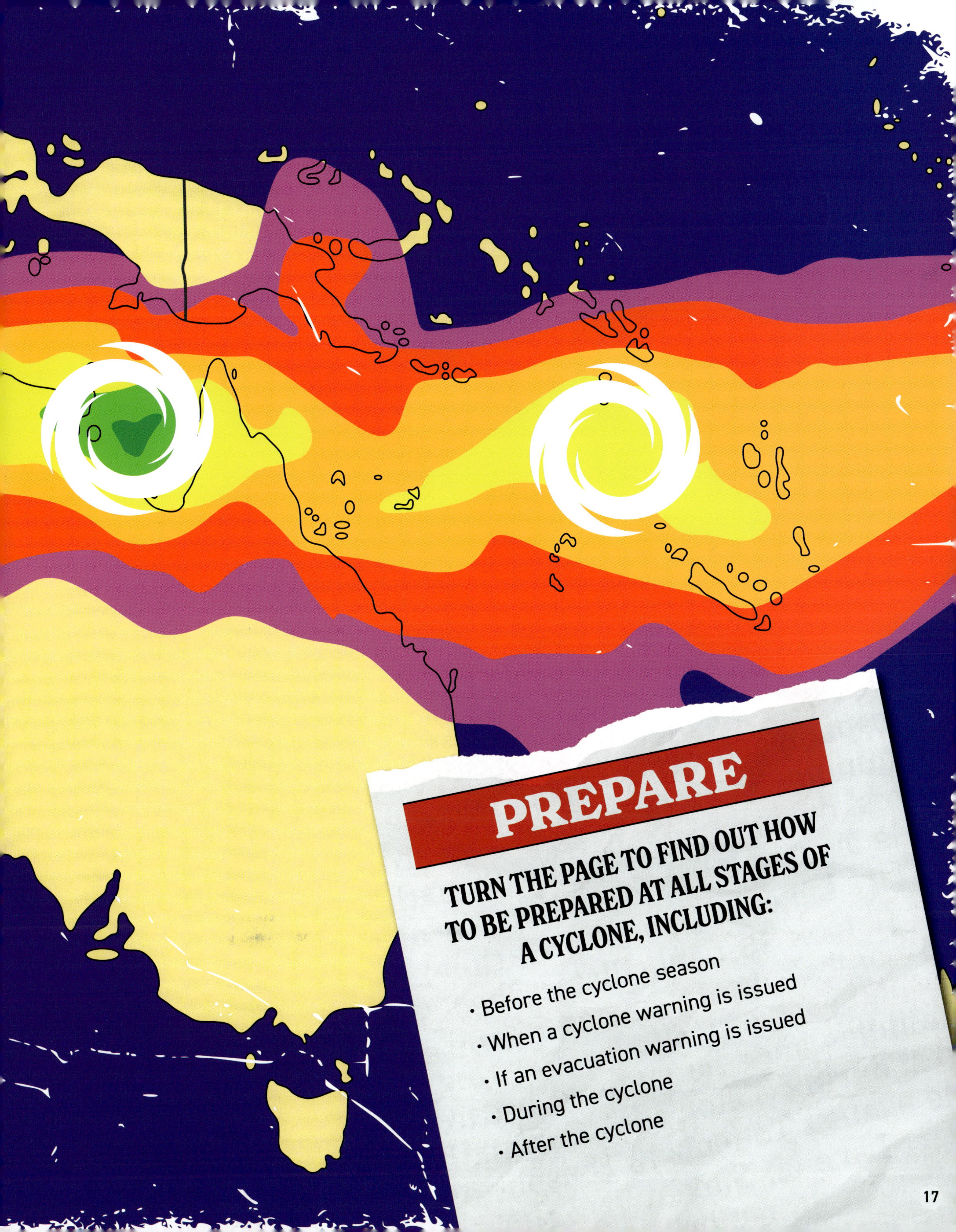
PREPARE
TURN THE PAGE TO FIND OUT HOW TO BE PREPARED AT ALL STAGES OF A CYCLONE, INCLUDING:
• Before the cyclone season
• When a cyclone warning is issued
• If an evacuation warning is issued
• During the cyclone
• After the cyclone

THINGS TO CONSIDER

BEFORE THE CYCLONE SEASON

Residents in cyclone areas should always make sure their homes have been built to cyclone standards and are secure. This includes attending to their yards and any surrounding trees.

They should have an emergency kit prepared, and for those residents who live near the coast, they need to know their safest high ground shelter.

IF A CYCLONE WARNING IS ISSUED

Firstly, residents should tie down boats, trailers and any loose material around their properties, such as trampolines. As well as checking their emergency kits, they should fill their car up with petrol and then park the car somewhere safe.

Often people collect important documents and some belongings, in case they need to evacuate, such as extra clothes, medications and special mementos. If possible, board up windows and stay inside the strongest part of the house with your pets. Maintain contact with neighbours and tune into the local news or radio for updates.

IF AN EVACUATION WARNING IS ISSUED

Sometimes evacuation is necessary. Official advice is given on local radio and television news regarding the safe routes, where to evacuate to and when it is time to evacuate. Always dress in clothes that will be comfortable for the days ahead, including covered shoes. Before leaving your home, turn off the power, gas and water and lock up, taking your evacuation and emergency kits.

WHAT TO DO WITH YOUR PETS

Whenever possible, your pets should always go with you. However, if you are being evacuated to an emergency shelter, it's generally suggested that you leave your pets somewhere safe inside your home, with enough food and water for ten days.

AT VARIOUS TIMES:

DURING THE CYCLONE

Always stay inside, either at home or at a designated emergency shelter. If you lose power, listen to a battery-operated radio for updates. If you need to protect yourself from falling debris, hide under strong tables or mattresses. After the cyclone, always wait for an official all clear from emergency services before leaving your home.

AFTER THE CYCLONE

Only go outside once it's safe. Stay away from fallen power lines and any storm surge water or floodwater. Never cross a flooded road in your car. Listen to local radio for advice.

CLEANING UP

IMPORTANT

CAUTION

- Always wear protective clothing
- Be aware of the food that you're eating and if it has spoiled
- Beware of hazardous materials
- Councils may help with cleanups

After a storm, the cleanup begins. This can be exhausting and emotionally stressful, depending on how much you've lost. Local authorities continue to advise during this time.

AFTERMATH

AFTER THE STORM

- Houses need to be repaired. Some houses will need to be demolished.
- Businesses might be closed for days after a storm. It's important to have emergency food and supplies on hand.
- Power supplies might be impacted.
- Report anything dangerous such as fallen power lines.
- Farmers will need to dispose of animals killed in the cyclone.

WILD WEATHER AND WILDLIFE

During a cyclone, local wildlife is often killed, displaced or injured. Some creatures will be on the move, so keep an eye out for snakes.

It is generally advised to leave all native wildlife alone, as they will recover and re-establish themselves in their habitat. However, if you do find an injured animal, contact your local branch of WIRES (Wildlife Information, Rescue and Education Service).

EMERGENCY SERVICES

In Australia, emergency services workers might be either volunteers or employees of government organisations.

During a tropical cyclone, police, paramedics and the fire brigade assist in emergencies.

Across Australia, over 44,000 SES volunteers play a vital role in helping communities prepare for, respond to and recover from emergencies.

LONG TERM IMPACTS

The impact of a tropical cyclone continues well after the storm is over.

HEALTH IMPACTS

Studies show that people who have survived a natural disaster, such as a cyclone, are prone to depression and PTSD. Along with their memories of the storm, the loss of their homes and personal effects and the ongoing financial burdens can cause great emotional distress.

ECONOMIC IMPACTS

The cost of a tropical cyclone is high. Along with destructive winds, there may be flooding and storm surges. The cleanup costs incurred are astronomical, and there is a serious impact on industries such as tourism and agriculture.

ENVIRONMENTAL IMPACTS

Cyclones cause damage to natural environments that can take decades to repair. In 2016, Cyclone Yasi caused damage across 89,000 square kilometres of the Great Barrier Reef. This area of the reef had been recovering from Cyclone Larry, only five years earlier.

Cyclone Yasi

QLD, 2011

DAMAGE INCLUDED

- The movement of coral boulders and the destruction of coral beds
- Movement of sand beds, changing the shape of the reef
- Destruction of sea grass beds
- Destruction of animal habitats, which impacted breeding cycles

AUSTRALIA'S WORST TROPICAL CYCLONES

Australia has experienced more than its fair share of tropical cyclones and too many to mention here. But the following Category 5 cyclones left their mark on each town and its residents.

CYCLONE MAHINA

Australia's deadliest tropical cyclone in recorded history was Cyclone Mahina. The cyclone was a category 5 that hit Princess Charlotte Bay in March 1899, killing over 300 people, many from local pearling vessels. Eight pearling vessels and 100 smaller luggers were anchored in the bay at the time of the cyclone. Overnight, half the fleet was destroyed.

The huge seas produced surges that swept inland. While it's not known for sure, some reports said that local Aboriginal people were washed out to sea.

CYCLONE MACKAY

Category 4, Cyclone Mackay hit the Queensland town of Mackay on 20 January 1918. The rest of the world didn't know about the disaster for five days, as it wiped out communication lines to and from the area.

Hurricane Katrina

One of the world's most memorable and devastating tropical cyclones in recent years was Hurricane Katrina. In 2005, this Category 5 Hurricane hit the eastern seaboard of the USA. The state of Louisiana was hit particularly hard, with the New Orleans levy breaking and flooding 80% of the city. The hurricane claimed approximately 1,390 lives and over a million people needed temporary shelter. With $125 billion US dollars in damages, Katrina was the costliest hurricane in US history.

Australia quickly learned a lot about emergency planning from Katrina. Later that year, an even stronger cyclone hit the Queensland town of Innisfail. Unlike the residents of New Orleans, who only had 24 hours' notice, the residents of Innisfail were given three days to secure their homes and stock up on emergency supplies.

CYCLONE LARRY

Cyclone Larry was a ferocious category 5, but thanks to being prepared, all 18,000 residents of the town survived and power and water was mostly restored by the following day.

CYCLONE YASI

One of the worst cyclones to hit Queensland was Yasi, which originated in Fiji. It was predicted to hit Cairns, so even hospital patients were evacuated. However, Yasi made landfall in Mission Beach, 50 kilometres south of Innisfail, so while the region was badly hit, Cairns and Innisfail were spared the worst of that monster storm.

Innisfail in Queensland is particularly prone to tropical cyclones. In 1918, one unnamed cyclone tore through the town leaving only 12 houses standing.

AUSTRALIA'S MOST DEVASTATING CHRISTMAS

On Christmas Day, 1974, Cyclone Tracy hit Darwin, in Australia's Northern Territory. It killed 66 people and destroyed 80% of the city. Over half the population of Darwin's 43,000 residents were left homeless.

Cyclone Tracy was one of Australia's worst ever natural disasters and left an indelible mark of the psyche on the nation. While most Australians woke to celebrate Christmas Day on 25 December, images of Darwin and its traumatised residents were being broadcast across our television screens.

POST-CYCLONE LESSONS

Cyclone Tracy was pivotal in the management of issues in cyclone-prone areas throughout Australia. It highlighted the need for improved disaster management, emergency responses and public awareness.

In 1974, cyclone-resistant housing construction practices were unregulated. The different building methods that have been used since mean that Darwin would withstand a similar cyclone much better than it did with Cyclone Tracy.

Cyclone Tracy

FAST FACTS

- Cyclone Tracy had winds of around 250 kilometres per hour
- 66 people were killed, most by flying debris
- 650 people were injured
- 30,000 people were evacuated
- 25,000 people were left homeless
- 94% of housing was uninhabitable
- The cost of the cyclone in today's money was between \$2 billion and \$4 billion Australian dollars.

HOW CYCLONES GET THEIR NAMES

Tropical cyclones were first named in the mid-1890s by a meteorologist called Clement Wragge. Originally from England, Wragge was appointed Government Meteorologist in Queensland in 1887. Wragge had a sense of humour, so began giving cyclones names, working in alphabetical order, a system that ended up in use worldwide.

The Australian Bureau of Meteorology began officially naming cyclones in 1963 and, in January 1964, the first two cyclones were named Audrey and Bessie. Only female names were used until 1979.

Now, cyclones names are chosen from an approved list, alternating between male and female. If the cyclone first forms in another region and is named there it keeps its name even if it hits Australia. An example of that is Tropical Cyclone Yasi which was named in Fiji.

Cyclone names can be reused until they make landfall and then that name will be retired. Well-known and celebrity names are generally avoided, so a cyclone Taylor (Swift) is unlikely.

YOUR OWN CYCLONE

Did you know that the Bureau of Meteorology takes requests for names? There's a long wait list, but if you apply, your name might one day be a cyclone.

HOW CLIMATE CHANGE AFFECTS TROPICAL CYCLONES

While climate change has influenced the frequency of natural disasters, it will actually mean fewer tropical cyclones, due to the gap between the warmer oceans and cool atmosphere decreasing. But before we celebrate that, this also means that the cyclones that do occur will be more ferocious than ever before.

Cyclones of the FUTURE

FUTURE CYCLONES WILL HAVE

- Stronger winds
- Heavier rain
- As sea levels rise due to the melting ice caps and coastal erosion takes place, the cyclones will cause more flooding and larger tidal surges

GLOSSARY

DEBRIS
pieces left behind after a destructive event

EYE OF THE STORM
calm centre of a tropical cyclone

EYEWALL
damaging rainbands around the centre of the storm

INUNDATED
completely flooded

LEVEE
wall of concrete, soil or sand to stop water flowing onto land

LOW-PRESSURE SYSTEM
moist rising air that causes rain, storms and clouds

MONSOON
weather system of heavy rain and strong winds

PTSD
post-traumatic stress disorder, not uncommon after experiencing a traumatic event

SES
volunteer organisation that provides an essential role during severe weather events.

STORM TIDE
tsunami-like body of water that hits the coast, when a high tide coincides with a storm surge

STORM SURGE
storm surge is a rise in sea level that is typically about two to five metres higher than the normal tide level

PRONE TO
likely to experience

RESPITE
period of relief from a problem

TSUNAMI
flood of water across land caused by an earthquake

INDEX